Hot SPOTS

Anita Ganeri

Published 2011
First published in hardback 2010 by
A&C Black Publishers Ltd.
36 Soho Square, London, W1D 3QY

www.acblack.com

ISBN 978-1-4081-2685-1

Series consultant: Gill Matthews

This book is produced using paper that is made from wood grown in managed, sustainable forests. It is natural, renewable and recyclable. The logging and manufacturing processes conform to the environmental regulations of the country of origin.

Produced for A&C Black by Calcium. www.calciumcreative.co.uk

Printed and bound in China by C&C Offset Printing Co.

All the internet addresses given in this book were correct at the time of going to press. The author and publishers regret any inconvenience caused if addresses have changed or sites have ceased to exist, but can accept no responsibility for any such changes.

Acknowledgements

The publishers would like to thank the following for their kind permission to reproduce their photographs:

Cover: Shutterstock. **Pages:** Alamy Images: RIA Novosti 29t, Juergen Ritterbach 13; Dreamstime: Peter Hazlett 7t, Asther Lau Choon Siew 27b; Fotolia: Delphimages 8, Idreamphoto 27t, RM 12, TextArt 18b; Istockphoto: Luoman 10b; Shutterstock: John Arnold 11, Jason Bennee 22l, Eugene Berman 4t, George Burba 5, Bryan Busovicki 18-19t, Peter Gordon 9t, Amy Nichole Harris 19b, Thomas Heinze 14-15, Imagix 21, Debra James 26l, Kkaplin 28-29, Mark Lundborg 17b, Meiqianbao 7b, Holger Mette 9b, 22-23, Christian Musat 25t, Ostill 23b, Patrick Poendl 20t, Paul Prescott 25b, Dr. Morley Read 10-11t, Schalke fotografie/ Melissa Schalke 16br, Sarah Theophilus 20-21, Tororo Reaction 26-27, Vladimir Wrangel 24-25, Peter Zaharov 6-7, Zed Zapper 16-17, Jarno Gonzalez Zarraonandia 15b.

CONTENTS

AROUND THE WORLD

From baking hot deserts to snow-capped mountains, Planet Earth is packed with places to explore. With so many destinations to choose from, where do you begin?

To get your journey off to a flying start, we've picked 12 of the most amazing places on the planet. Get ready to battle your way through steamy rainforest and go scuba diving on a coral reef. If that's not exciting enough for you, try photographing a volcano that has been erupting almost non stop for the past 25 years!

VISIT THE AMAZING AMAZON RAINFOREST.

North America

8

6

7

4

3

5 South
America

Antarctica

See it before it's too late!

You'll have to hurry if you want to visit some of the places in this book. They're under threat because of the action of human beings. Some places are in danger from **global warming** or pollution. Others are being destroyed for their **resources**.

Why so special?

What makes these 12 places so special? The answer is that they are all record-breakers – from the longest river to the largest grassland and the highest waterfall. Of course, plenty of other "hotspots" have not made it on to our list, but be ready for the adventure of a lifetime! Use the map to help plot your course.

Map key

1 **Mount Everest**
  The highest mountain
2 **Tokyo**
  The biggest city
3 **Amazon rainforest**
  The biggest rainforest
4 **Angel Falls**
  The highest waterfall
5 **Lake Titicaca**
  The highest lake
6 **Great Plains**
  The largest grassland
7 **Kilauea**
  The most active volcano
8 **Greenland**
  The biggest island
9 **River Nile**
  The longest river
10 **Sahara Desert**
  The largest desert
11 **Great Barrier Reef**
  The longest coral reef
12 **Vostok**
  The coldest place

Europe

Asia

Africa

Australia

12

SEE THE FIERY FLAMES OF KILAUEA.

CLIMB TO THE TOP OF MOUNT EVEREST.

Head for Mount Everest on the border of Nepal and China, for a view of the Earth with a difference. At 8,848 metres (more than 29,000 ft) tall, Everest is the highest mountain on Earth.

Everest is part of the Himalayas mountain range, where all 14 of the world's highest peaks are found. If the weather isn't cloudy, you can fly right over the mountain. From the air, it's a breathtaking sight. Otherwise, you'll have to take your chances and climb to the **summit**.

TRAVELLERS' TIPS

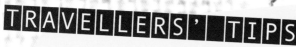

If you feel sick and dizzy, you might have altitude sickness. This is caused by the lack of **oxygen** high up on the mountain. In the worst cases, fluid can build up in your lungs and brain and kill you. The best thing is to climb at a slow, steady pace. But if you feel bad or have trouble breathing, get off the mountain quickly and go to a doctor.

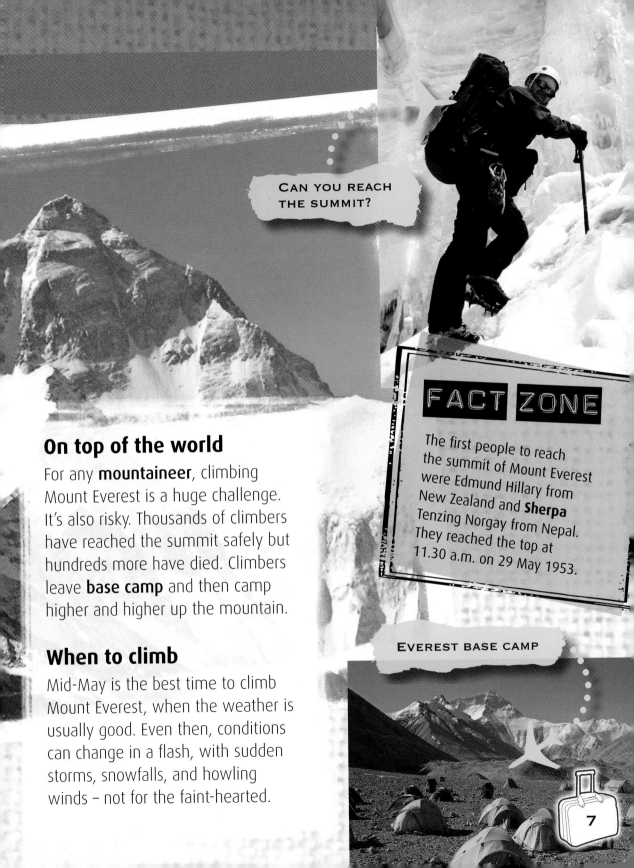

CAN YOU REACH THE SUMMIT?

FACT ZONE

The first people to reach the summit of Mount Everest were Edmund Hillary from New Zealand and **Sherpa** Tenzing Norgay from Nepal. They reached the top at 11.30 a.m. on 29 May 1953.

On top of the world

For any **mountaineer**, climbing Mount Everest is a huge challenge. It's also risky. Thousands of climbers have reached the summit safely but hundreds more have died. Climbers leave **base camp** and then camp higher and higher up the mountain.

When to climb

Mid-May is the best time to climb Mount Everest, when the weather is usually good. Even then, conditions can change in a flash, with sudden storms, snowfalls, and howling winds – not for the faint-hearted.

EVEREST BASE CAMP

TOKYO

There is one thing you just can't miss in Japan's capital, Tokyo, and that is people! Tokyo is the most crowded city in the world – it has 35 million **inhabitants**. It gets even busier in the day as people **commute** into the city to work.

Incredibly, Tokyo was once a quiet fishing village on the shores of Tokyo Bay. Today, it is one of the world's most important **financial** centres and home to the Japanese government.

EXPLORE THE INCREDIBLE CITY OF TOKYO.

TRAVELLERS' TIPS

Some things to do:
- Buy some fish at the Tsukiji Fish Market.
- Take a stroll through the gardens of the Imperial Palace, home of the royal family.
- Have a picnic in Ueno Park in spring when the cherry blossoms are blooming.
- Take a train to Odaiba, an **artificial** island built in the bay.

BUY DINNER AT TSJUKIJI
FISH MARKET.

FACT ZONE

Most of the buildings in Tokyo are new and modern. This is because the old city was destroyed by an earthquake in 1923, and then destroyed again during World War II.

Getting around

There is something for everyone in Tokyo, from busy shopping centres, to incredible high-rise buildings and peaceful parks. The best way to get about the city is by train – a ride on the high-speed "**bullet train**" is an amazing experience. Avoid travelling during **rush hour**. The trains get so crowded, you'll struggle even to find a place to stand!

TAKE A RIDE ON
A BULLET TRAIN.

It would take at least a month to walk from one end of the Amazon rainforest to the other. Not surprisingly, this is the largest rainforest on Earth. It is almost the same size as Australia.

The rainforest grows along the banks of the mighty River Amazon in South America. The river is a record-breaker in its own right. More water flows along the Amazon than any other river on Earth.

SEE THE AMAZON RAINFOREST FROM THE AIR.

See it before it's too late!

An area of the Amazon rainforest the size of four football pitches is chopped down EVERY MINUTE.

Wonderful wildlife

The rainforest is hot and **humid**, and has rain almost every day – these are perfect conditions for plants and animals to live in. The Amazon's home to one in ten of all the known **species** in the world. There are speedy jaguars, sleepy **sloths**, poison dart frogs, colourful **macaws**, and scary **piranhas**, among many others. This isn't a place for anyone scared of "creepy crawlies". Insects are constantly buzzing and zipping about. Scientists think that some 2.5 million species of insects live in the rainforest, and about a third of these are ants.

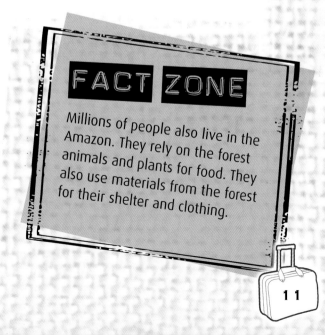

FACT ZONE

Millions of people also live in the Amazon. They rely on the forest animals and plants for food. They also use materials from the forest for their shelter and clothing.

CATCH IT SOON – IT MIGHT NOT BE HERE FOR LONG...

ANGEL FALLS

Getting to the Angel Falls isn't easy. They're hidden deep inside the Canaima National Park in Venezuela, South America.

To get to the Falls, fly to Canaima. Then take a five-hour canoe ride along the river. Finally, hike for an hour through thick rainforest to the base of the Falls. But the truly breathtaking views of the world's highest waterfall make the long trek worthwhile.

ANGEL FALLS – WOW!

TRAVELLERS' TIPS

Get ready for a soaking if you are heading for Angel Falls. Plunging 979 metres (3,212 ft) off the edge of a cliff, they're so high that the water turns to mist long before it hits the ground. The mist can be felt over a kilometre away. The driest time to visit is between December and April.

Amazing discovery

Angel Falls are named after American pilot, Jimmy Angel, who discovered them in 1933. Before this, only the local people knew about them. Angel was searching for a gold mine when he flew over the Falls. He returned four years later and landed on top of them, but his plane's wheels sank into the boggy ground and he couldn't take off again. Instead, he had to climb down the mountain and walk for 11 days to the nearest village. It was another 33 years before his plane was rescued.

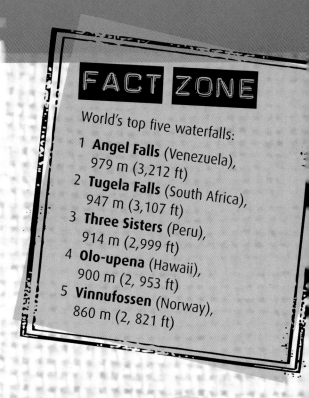

FACT ZONE

World's top five waterfalls:

1 **Angel Falls** (Venezuela), 979 m (3,212 ft)
2 **Tugela Falls** (South Africa), 947 m (3,107 ft)
3 **Three Sisters** (Peru), 914 m (2,999 ft)
4 **Olo-upena** (Hawaii), 900 m (2, 953 ft)
5 **Vinnufossen** (Norway), 860 m (2, 821 ft)

THE PLANE THAT TOOK JIMMY ANGEL TO THE FALLS.

LAKE TITICACA

Don't miss Lake Titicaca. Surrounded by the snow-capped Andes Mountains, it's a stunning sight. At more than 3,800 metres (12,470 ft) above sea level, it's also the world's highest **navigable** lake.

You can hire a boat and guide to explore the lake, though swimming is definitely not recommended! The lake's filled by water from melting **glaciers** and is freezing cold.

See it before it's too late!

Lake Titicaca is being polluted by waste from the towns and cities growing up on the shore. This is putting the Uru's traditional lifestyle under threat. The Uru rely on fish from the lake for food and their living. But pollution is poisoning both the fish and the Uru people.

THE BEAUTIFUL LAKE TITICACA

14

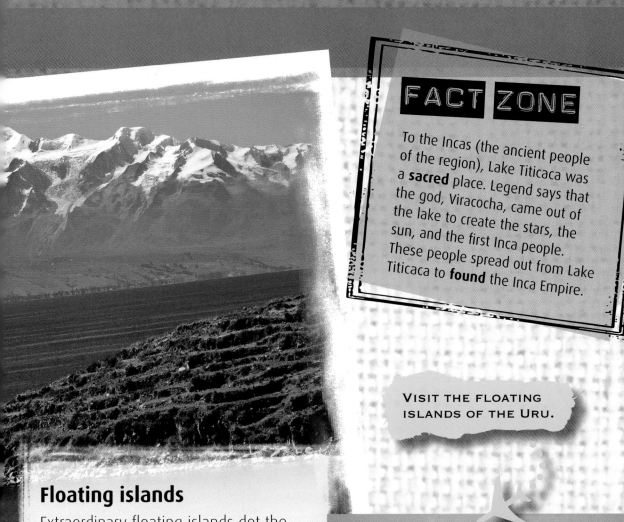

To the Incas (the ancient people of the region), Lake Titicaca was a **sacred** place. Legend says that the god, Viracocha, came out of the lake to create the stars, the sun, and the first Inca people. These people spread out from Lake Titicaca to **found** the Inca Empire.

VISIT THE FLOATING ISLANDS OF THE URU.

Floating islands

Extraordinary floating islands dot the lake. They're the home of the Uru people who've lived on the lake for centuries. The Uru build the islands from the totora reeds that grow along the lakeshore. They also use bundles of reeds to make their banana-shaped fishing boats. A boat lasts for about six months before the reeds start to rot. These handy reeds are also burned as fuel, used as animal food, and made into rope and baskets.

15

GREAT PLAINS

From the air, it is easy to see why the Great Plains hold the record for being the world's largest grassland. Also called the Prairies, they stretch for more than 1.4 million square kilometres (550,543 sq. miles) from southern Canada, down through the USA and into northern Mexico.

Huge areas of the Prairies have been turned into fields, where farmers grow more wheat, oats, barley, rye, and maize than anywhere else on Earth. Massive machines are used to harvest the grain. Important supplies of oil and coal are also found on the Prairies.

See it before it's too late!

Hundreds of years ago, more than 60 million American bison grazed on the Great Plains. Some herds were so big that it took an hour or more for them to cross a river. But hunters killed so many bison that they almost became **extinct**. Today, only about 30,000 survive and they live in specially protected parks and nature reserves.

AMERICAN BISON – AWESOME!

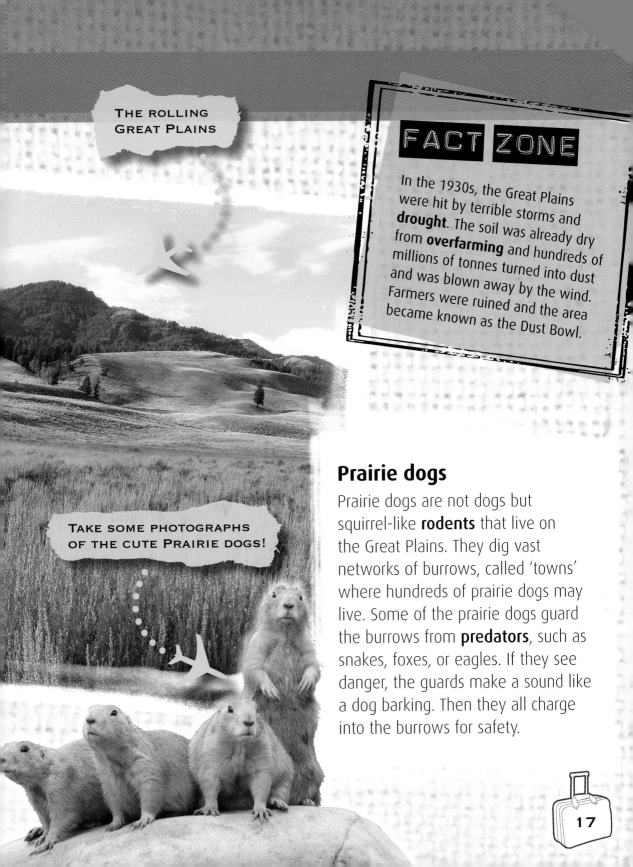

THE ROLLING
GREAT PLAINS

TAKE SOME PHOTOGRAPHS
OF THE CUTE PRAIRIE DOGS!

FACT ZONE

In the 1930s, the Great Plains were hit by terrible storms and **drought**. The soil was already dry from **overfarming** and hundreds of millions of tonnes turned into dust and was blown away by the wind. Farmers were ruined and the area became known as the Dust Bowl.

Prairie dogs

Prairie dogs are not dogs but squirrel-like **rodents** that live on the Great Plains. They dig vast networks of burrows, called 'towns' where hundreds of prairie dogs may live. Some of the prairie dogs guard the burrows from **predators**, such as snakes, foxes, or eagles. If they see danger, the guards make a sound like a dog barking. Then they all charge into the burrows for safety.

KILAUEA

Expect fireworks on a trip to Kilauea. This record-breaking volcano on the island of Hawaii is the most **active** volcano on Earth. Incredibly, it has been erupting almost non stop since 1983.

The word 'Kilauea' means 'spreading' and the volcano certainly lives up to its name. Every day, it spurts out huge amounts of **lava** that cools and turns into rock. The lava has added extra rocky land, the size of 300 football pitches, to the island.

TRAVELLERS' TIPS

Also worth a visit is Mauna Loa, another record-breaking volcano on Hawaii. It's the world's largest active volcano. From its base on the sea bed, it stands over 9 kilometres (5½ miles) tall. Mauna Loa last erupted in 1984, but scientists are watching it carefully in case it shows signs of erupting again.

MAUNA LOA

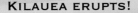

FACT ZONE

Local legend says that a goddess called Pele lives inside Kilauea, and the volcano erupts when she is angry. So people throw offerings of berries, coins, fruit, and flowers into the crater in the hope that this will keep Pele happy and the volcano quiet.

MAKE SURE YOU DRIVE AROUND THE LAVA ON CRATER RIM DRIVE!

Volcano visiting

You can actually drive right around the **crater** of Kilauea on a road, called Crater Rim Drive. On your way up, the road takes you through rainforests and rocky lava fields. Parts of the road regularly get buried by lava so check that they're clear before setting off. You might prefer to walk up to the crater along the official trails, but you'll need to wear sturdy walking boots. Lava is extremely sharp and can cut ordinary shoes to shreds.

GREENLAND

The first sight of Greenland comes as a shock. As your plane flies in to land, there's hardly any "green" to be seen. Greenland is mostly covered by a sheet of ice that, in places, is an incredible 4 kilometres (2½ miles) thick. The ice is so heavy that the ground underneath it has dipped.

Look out for the glaciers that flow from the ice sheet into the sea. Then watch them break up into huge floating icebergs.

MOST OF GREENLAND IS COVERED IN ICE.

See it before it's too late!

Global warming is melting Greenland's ice at an alarming rate. If the ice melts completely, it will cause the sea level around the world to rise. This will mean disaster for low-lying countries, such as Bangladesh. But it's not all bad news. The warmer weather means that Greenlanders can now grow vegetables, such as carrots and broccoli, for the first time.

SEE ICEBERGS MELT OFF
THE COAST OF GREENLAND.

VISIT NUUK, THE CAPITAL
OF GREENLAND.

Cold climate

Wrap up warm if you're visiting Greenland. It has a very harsh, cold **climate**. Even in summer, the temperature is a chilly 10°C (50°F). Most Greenlanders live along the south-west coast where it's "warmer". Many earn their living by fishing for shrimps.

What's in a name?

So who decided to call this white, icy territory Greenland? It was named by the Vikings who moved there from Iceland in the 10th century AD. They hoped that the name would entice other settlers to the island.

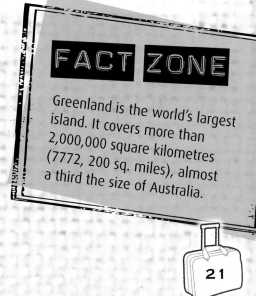

FACT ZONE

Greenland is the world's largest island. It covers more than 2,000,000 square kilometres (7772, 200 sq. miles), almost a third the size of Australia.

RIVER NILE

The best way to see the River Nile is by boat. You can take your pick from a luxury cruise liner or a felucca, a traditional sailing boat.

The Nile is the longest river in the world, and has been used for transport since ancient times. It flows across North Africa for 6,695 kilometres (4,160 miles), from Burundi to the Mediterranean Sea. As the river flows through Egypt, you can sit back and enjoy spotting the pyramids and other sights.

THE AWE-INSPIRING STATUES OF ABU SIMBEL

TRAVELLERS' TIPS

Look out for the temples of Abu Simbel on a hill above Lake Nasser. In the 1960s, the temples were in danger of being drowned when the lake was made. Engineers cut the temples into huge blocks, dragged them uphill, and rebuilt them on a new site. It was an amazing feat.

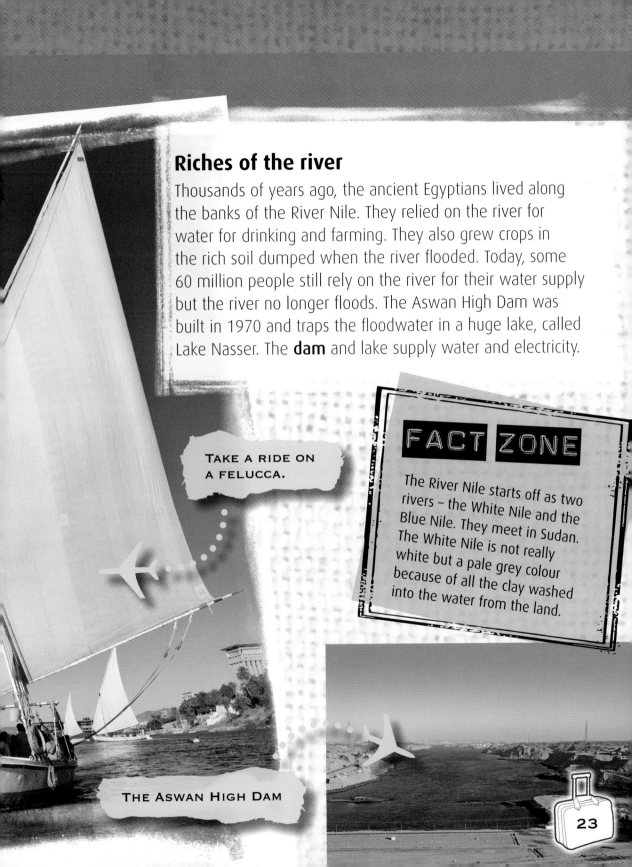

Riches of the river

Thousands of years ago, the ancient Egyptians lived along the banks of the River Nile. They relied on the river for water for drinking and farming. They also grew crops in the rich soil dumped when the river flooded. Today, some 60 million people still rely on the river for their water supply but the river no longer floods. The Aswan High Dam was built in 1970 and traps the floodwater in a huge lake, called Lake Nasser. The **dam** and lake supply water and electricity.

TAKE A RIDE ON A FELUCCA.

FACT ZONE

The River Nile starts off as two rivers – the White Nile and the Blue Nile. They meet in Sudan. The White Nile is not really white but a pale grey colour because of all the clay washed into the water from the land.

THE ASWAN HIGH DAM

SAHARA DESERT

Imagine the Sahara Desert and you probably think of a huge sea of sand. The Sahara is enormous, almost as large as the USA and the biggest desert in the world. It's only partly sandy, however, with **sand dunes** as high as 60-storey buildings. But large parts are also rocky, pebbly, salty, and mountainous.

Exploring the desert is tough-going. After all, it is one of the harshest places on Earth. Temperatures range from scorching hot in the daytime to freezing cold at night, and there's no rain for months on end. You'd better take light clothes and a sun hat for the day and a warm jumper for the night.

THE INCREDIBLE SAND DUNES OF THE SAHARA DESERT

TRAVELLERS' TIPS

Don't forget to take plenty of water on your desert trek. Without water, you will quickly get **dehydrated** and could die of thirst in just two days. You need to drink at least nine litres of water a day to stay alive in the desert.

WILL YOU SPOT A FENNEL FOX?

Amazing desert animals

If you're lucky you may come across some desert wildlife. Animals living in the Sahara Desert have special features to help them survive. The fennec fox's huge ears are lined with hair to keep out dust and sand. The fox uses its ears to listen out for its **prey** of **locusts** and beetles. It also loses heat through its ears to stay cool.

Camels are ideal desert animals. They can go for many days without drinking and use the fat stored in their humps for food. They also have two sets of eyelashes and can close their nostrils to keep out the sand. They have webbed feet, like sandshoes, for walking over the soft sand without sinking. If you get a chance to have a camel ride, watch out for it spitting – camels can be grumpy!

EXPLORE THE DESERT BY CAMEL – IF YOU DARE!

FACT ZONE

About 6,000 years ago, the Sahara was wet and green, with giraffes, crocodiles, elephants, and hippos roaming across it.

GREAT BARRIER REEF

Diving into the Great Barrier Reef, you enter a magical, underwater world. The world's largest coral reef lies off the north-east coast of Australia. It stretches for more than 2,600 kilometres (1,615 miles) and is so big it can be seen from space.

FLY OVER THE GREAT BARRIER REEF.

DIVE UNDERWATER TO SEE THE REEF UP CLOSE.

See it before it's too late!

Like reefs all over the world, the Great Barrier Reef is in serious danger. Human activities, such as fishing, mining, and pollution, are destroying the reef. One of the worst threats is coral **bleaching**, caused by global warming. As the sea gets warmer, the living coral turns white and dies. Eventually, the reef crumbles away.

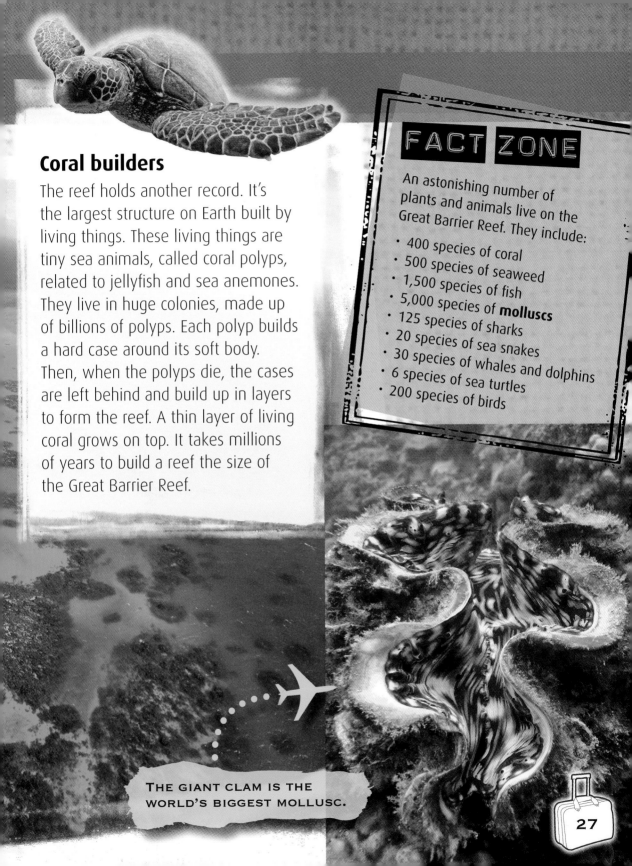

Coral builders

The reef holds another record. It's the largest structure on Earth built by living things. These living things are tiny sea animals, called coral polyps, related to jellyfish and sea anemones. They live in huge colonies, made up of billions of polyps. Each polyp builds a hard case around its soft body. Then, when the polyps die, the cases are left behind and build up in layers to form the reef. A thin layer of living coral grows on top. It takes millions of years to build a reef the size of the Great Barrier Reef.

FACT ZONE

An astonishing number of plants and animals live on the Great Barrier Reef. They include:

- 400 species of coral
- 500 species of seaweed
- 1,500 species of fish
- 5,000 species of **molluscs**
- 125 species of sharks
- 20 species of sea snakes
- 30 species of whales and dolphins
- 6 species of sea turtles
- 200 species of birds

THE GIANT CLAM IS THE WORLD'S BIGGEST MOLLUSC.

VOSTOK

No other place on Earth is as cold as Vostok in eastern Antarctica. You will need to wear many layers of warm clothes to survive your visit. At this Russian research base, temperatures fall as low as –89.3°C (–129°F) – about ten times colder than the inside of a deep freezer!

About 25 scientists live on the base in summer, when temperatures rise to around –30°C (–22°F). They drill **ice cores** and study the climate. In winter, just 13 tough scientists stay to cope with the cold, howling winds, and weeks of darkness.

WRAP UP AND HEAD FOR ANTARCTICA.

TRAVELLERS' TIPS

In freezing Antarctica, frostbite is a real danger. This is when your skin and flesh get so cold that they start to freeze and die – sometimes turning black! Your fingers, feet, ears, and nose are most at risk. If the skin starts looking waxy then goes numb, try **thawing** it out with warm water.

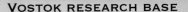

Icy Antarctica

Almost all of Antarctica is covered by an enormous ice sheet which, in places, is almost 5 kilometres (3 miles) thick. Mountains and volcanoes lie underneath the ice. They were buried millions of years ago. Some of the volcanoes are still active. Around Antarctica lies the Southern Ocean. In winter, a large part of the ocean freezes over, making the size of Antarctica twice as big.

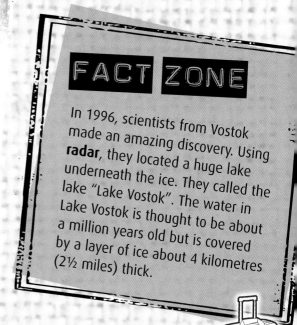

FACT ZONE

In 1996, scientists from Vostok made an amazing discovery. Using **radar**, they located a huge lake underneath the ice. They called the lake "Lake Vostok". The water in Lake Vostok is thought to be about a million years old but is covered by a layer of ice about 4 kilometres (2½ miles) thick.

29

GLOSSARY

active a volcano that is still erupting

artificial made by people, not natural

base camp the first camp on the way up a mountain

bleaching when something goes white and dies

bullet train a very fast train in Japan

climate the type of weather a place has over a long period of time

commute to travel into and out of a place for work

crater the pit at the top of a volcano

dam a long barrier built across a river

dehydrated feeling ill because of a lack of water

drought a long period without rain

extinct a plant or animal that has died out for ever

financial to do with money

found to set up or start

glaciers areas of ice that extend from ice sheets and mountains

global warming the increase in the Earth's temperature

humid damp or moist

ice cores long sticks of ice drilled out of the ground that tell scientists about the past climate

inhabitants the people who live in a place

lava molten rock flowing from a volcano

locusts large desert insects, like grasshoppers

macaws large parrots that live in the rainforest

molluscs a marine animal with a shell, such as a clam or snail

mountaineer a person who climbs mountains

navigable able to be crossed by boat

overfarming farming a piece of land for too long, or too much

oxygen a gas in the air that humans and animals need to breathe

piranhas fish, famous for their sharp teeth

predators animals that hunt other animals for food

prey animals that are hunted by other animals for food

radar an instrument that detects distant objects

resources valuable products from a place, such as oil or fish

rodents a type of mammal, such as squirrels, mice, and rats

rush hour busy times of the day when people travel to and from work

sacred holy

sand dunes sand that has been blown into a ridge by the wind

Sherpa someone who lives near the Himalayas and is an experienced mountain climber

sloths animals that spend most of their time asleep in the trees

species types of animals or plants

summit the top of a mountain

thawing warming something up

FURTHER INFORMATION

Websites

Find out about places around the world at:
www.worldatlas.com

Learn about places that are in danger at:
www.edgeofexistence.org

For information about the world and its wildlife, click on:
www.nationalgeographic.com

Books

Horrible Geography: Planet in Peril by Anita Ganeri, Scholastic (2009).

Whitaker's World of Facts 2011 by Russel Ash, A&C Black (2010).

Wow! Earth by Dorling Kindersley (2009).

INDEX